SUPERSTARS!

THE STARS OF
THE HUNGER GAMES

SUPERSTARS!

THE STARS OF
THE HUNGER GAMES

PRODUCED BY

SCOUT
BOOKS & MEDIA

President Susan Knopf
Writer Sarah Christensen Fu
Book designed by Greg Wozney, Greg Wozney Design
Cover designed by Brian Greenberg, Andrij Borys Associates, LLC
Editorial intern Chelsea M. Burris
Special thanks Andrij Borys/Andrij Borys Associates, LLC;
Michael Centore; Annemarie Redmond Design, Inc.

HOME ENTERTAINMENT

Publisher Jim Childs
Vice President, Brand & Digital Strategy Steven Sandonato
Executive Director Marketing Services Carol Pittard
Executive Director, Retail & Special Sales Tom Mifsud
Executive Publishing Director Joy Butts
Director, Bookazine Development & Marketing Laura Adam
Finance Director Glenn Buonocore
Associate Publishing Director Megan Pearlman
Associate General Counsel Helen Wan
Assistant Director, Special Sales Ilene Schreider
Brand Manager, Product Marketing Nina Fleishman Reed
Associate Prepress Manager Alex Voznesenskiy
Associate Production Manager Kimberly Marshall

Editorial Director Stephen Koepp
Copy Chief Rina Bander
Design Manager Anne-Michelle Gallero

SPECIAL THANKS TO Katherine Barnet, Jeremy Biloon, Stephanie
Braga, Dana Campolattaro, Susan Chodakiewicz, Rose Cirrincione,
Natalie Ebel, Assu Etsubneh, Mariana Evans, Jacqueline Fitzgerald,
Christine Font, Susan Hettleman, Hillary Hirsch, David Kahn, Amy
Mangus, Nina Mistry, Dave Rozzelle, Ricardo Santiago, Gina Scauzillo,
Adriana Tierno, Vanessa Wu

Published by Time Home Entertainment Inc.
135 West 50th Street · New York, NY 10020

ISBN 10: 1-61893-349-3
ISBN 13: 978-1-61893-349-2

We welcome your comments and suggestions about Time Home Entertainment Books. Please write to us at: Time Home Entertainment Books,
Attention: Book Editors, P.O. Box 11016, Des Moines, IA 50336-1016
If you would like to order any of our hardcover Collector's Edition books,
please call us at 1-800-327-6388, Monday through Friday, 7 a.m. to 8
p.m., or Saturday, 7 a.m. to 6 p.m., Central Time.

1 QGC 13

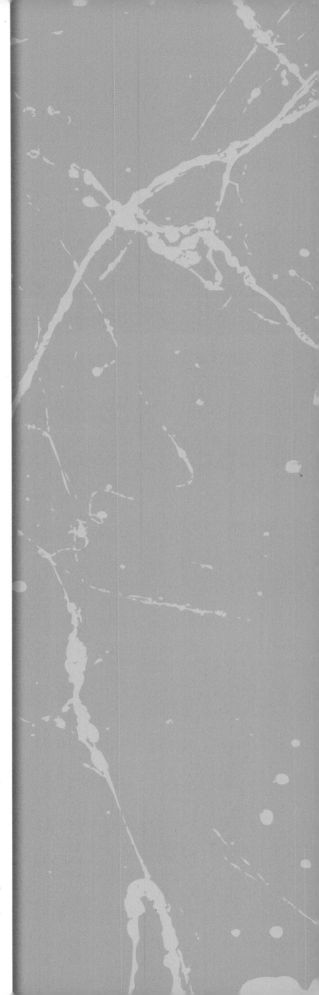

TABLE OF CONTENTS

Movie MAGIC

Sometimes magic happens when a group of actors come together in a movie. The actors in *The Hunger Games* embody the characters in memorable and compelling ways, and they light up the screen and captivate fans everywhere. Stars Jennifer Lawrence, Josh Hutcherson, and Liam Hemsworth seem made for their roles. They also seem made for each other, with perfect onscreen chemistry and offscreen camaraderie. It's hard to think of one of them without also thinking of the others; this is what's called an iconic cast. And they're not the first group of young actors to make this kind of impact.

Liam, Jen, and Josh have star power!

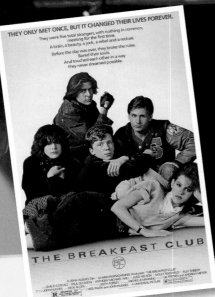

In the 1980s, a group of young actors became known as the "Brat Pack." This group included Emilio Estevez, Anthony Michael Hall, Rob Lowe, Andrew McCarthy, Demi Moore, Judd Nelson, Molly Ringwald, and Ally Sheedy. These actors will always be associated with the classic movies they starred in—The Breakfast Club and St. Elmo's Fire—and with one another.

Anthony Michael Hall, Molly Ringwald, Ally Sheedy, and Judd Nelson celebrate the 25th anniversary of The Breakfast Club.

Robert Pattinson, Kristen Stewart, and Taylor Lautner put their handprints in cement at Grauman's Chinese Theatre in Hollywood.

The love triangle between Bella, Edward, and Jacob in the Twilight movies was otherworldly. But it was also the real-life actors Kristen Stewart, Robert Pattinson, and Taylor Lautner who made our hearts race. This iconic cast starred in all four Twilight movies, and will always be thought of together.

Meet
JENNIFER LAWRENCE

Full name: Jennifer Shrader Lawrence
Goes by: Jen
Birth date: August 15, 1990
Zodiac sign: Leo
Height: 5' 7"

Hobbies: Playing basketball and the guitar
Born in: Louisville, Kentucky
Parents: Karen and Gary Lawrence
Siblings: Two older brothers, Ben and Blaine
Lives in: Santa Monica, California

The skyline of Louisville, Kentucky—where Jen was born.

Jen playing guitar in The House at the End of the Street.

9

One of the KIDS!

Born on August 15, 1990, Jen grew up with her parents Karen and Gary Lawrence and older brothers Ben and Blaine.

Jen attended Kammerer Middle School in Louisville. She confided to the *Los Angeles Times* that she "always felt dumber than everybody else" in school, but she graduated from high school two years early with a 3.9 GPA. That makes her one smart cookie!

After playing Desdemona in a local production of *Othello*, Jen knew she wanted to make acting her career and convinced her parents to take her to New York City. She quickly found a talent agent, and soon landed her first acting role.

Jen says:

"Growing up, I lived 15 minutes away from a horse farm, and I went there almost every day. My brothers were into fishing, but I was all about the horses." *(Seventeen)* And this Louisville native has gotten to use this experience with horses in her career; one of Jen's co-stars in *Winter's Bone* was a horse.

Jen with her Dance Cheer group

Didja know?

Jen's childhood nickname was "Nitro," because she was always so hyper-energetic!

Glam Fam: Jen and her parents at the Academy Awards.

Jen was 16 years old when she got her first big break—a role on *The Bill Engvall Show*. Playing Lauren, the outgoing, overachieving high school student, was a revelation to Jen. "I was out of the box, [thinking] I'm good at this. I can memorize a script from the first read-through. I can stand on my mark!" Jen confided to her hometown newspaper, the Louisville *Courier-Journal*. The show ran for three years and launched Jen's acting career.

JEN'S BIG BREAK!

"I had so much fun on that show, and we all became like family!"

Jen told *Under the Radar* magazine.

Jen says:

"Acting is something that makes me happier than ever, so if I could do this for the rest of my life, I'd be the happiest person on the planet!"

(Courier-Journal)

Young Artist Award Winner, 2009

Bill Engvall remembers thinking, while filming the show, "This girl is good. She's got it, she's got what it takes."

(Examiner.com)

Meet
JOSH HUTCHERSON

Yahoo Falls in Kentucky, near where Josh grew up.

Full name: Joshua Ryan Hutcherson
Birth date: October 2, 1992
Zodiac sign: Libra
Goes by: Josh
Height: 5' 7"
Hobbies: Playing sports, especially soccer, and building remote control cars
Born in: Union, Kentucky
Parents: Michelle Fightmaster and Chris Hutcherson
Siblings: A younger brother, Connor
Lives in: Josh lives part-time in California. When he's not on set or filming around the globe, he also lives part-time with his family in his hometown in Kentucky.

BOY OH BOY!

Such a cutie!

Josh Hutcherson was born in the small town of Union, Kentucky. That's less than two hours from Louisville, where Jen grew up, but Josh and Jen didn't meet until they were both actors. Josh's father, Christopher, works for the U.S. Environmental Protection Agency, and his mother, Michelle, used to work for Delta Air Lines— she now helps Josh with his career. He has a younger brother, Connor, who acted alongside Josh in the film *Little Manhattan* when he was nine and Josh was 13.

Josh knew he wanted to be an actor at age four, and he finally convinced his parents . . . five years later! Josh told *Portrait* magazine that he found an agent through the Yellow Pages when he was nine years old and sent in a photo of himself, and that's how he got his start. His family moved to California for a year so Josh could try acting.

Josh and his family at the Los Angeles premiere of Zathura (2005).

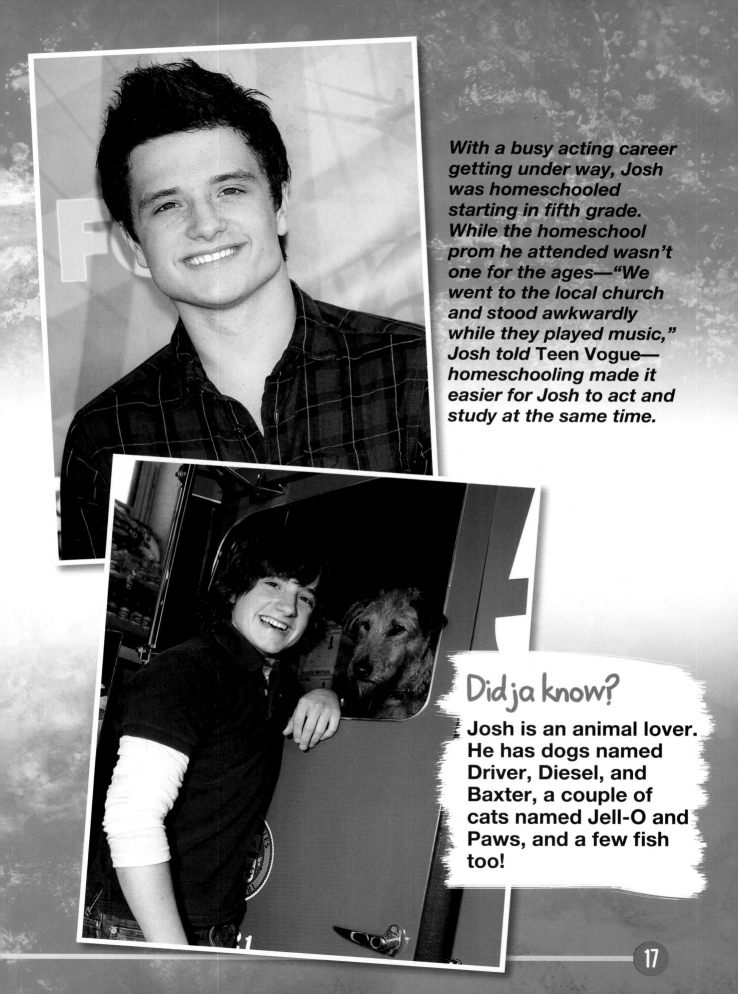

With a busy acting career getting under way, Josh was homeschooled starting in fifth grade. While the homeschool prom he attended wasn't one for the ages—"We went to the local church and stood awkwardly while they played music," Josh told Teen Vogue—homeschooling made it easier for Josh to act and study at the same time.

Didja know?

Josh is an animal lover. He has dogs named Driver, Diesel, and Baxter, a couple of cats named Jell-O and Paws, and a few fish too!

It may have taken Josh five years to convince his parents that he wanted to be an actor, but once he did, they supported him in a big way. The family moved to California for a year so Josh could try out "pilot season," a time when networks and studios cast first episodes, known as pilots, for new shows. It was a good move for Josh; he got a pilot for a show called *House Blend*. The show didn't make it, but later that year Josh acted in an episode of *ER*, and his career was under way.

JOSH'S BREAKTHROUGH

Josh played dog lover Charlie Logan in the warm-hearted television movie Miracle Dogs (Animal Planet, 2003). And he took to the road in a grandfather-grandson road trip movie called Wilder Days, *with co-stars Peter Falk and Tim Daly.*

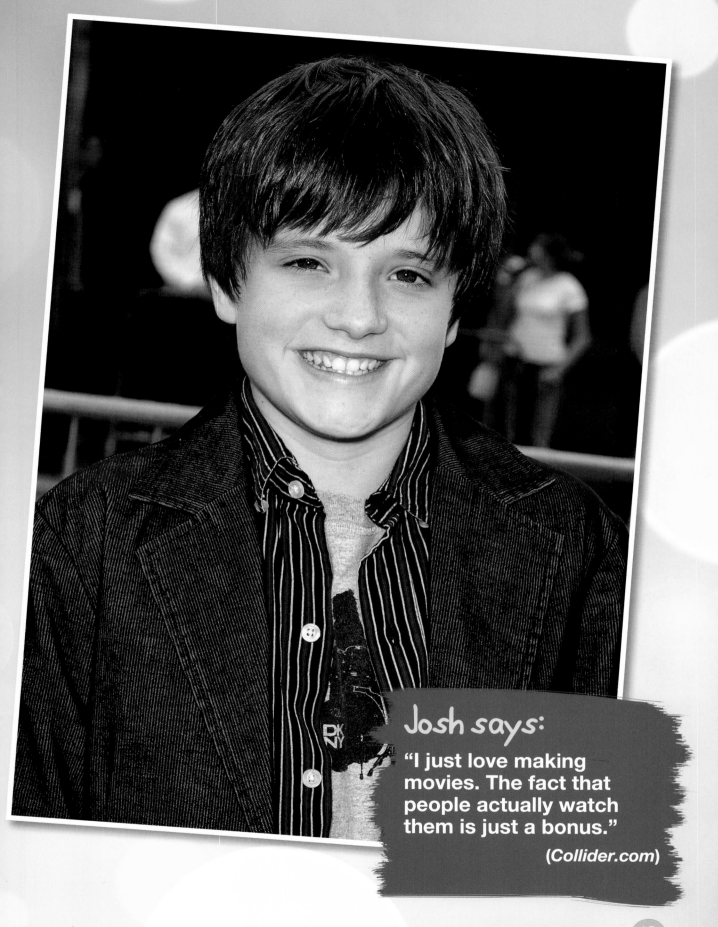

Josh says:

"I just love making movies. The fact that people actually watch them is just a bonus."

(Collider.com)

Meet
LIAM HEMSWORTH

Full name: Liam Hemsworth
Birth date: January 13, 1990
Zodiac sign: Capricorn
Goes by: Liam
Height: 6' 3"
Hobbies: Surfing, surfing, and surfing

Born in: Melbourne, Australia
Parents: Leonie and Craig Hemsworth
Siblings: Two older brothers, Chris and Luke
Lives in: Los Angeles, California
Engaged to: Miley Cyrus (but it's been on-again, off-again, so maybe, maybe not)

The Melbourne skyline—where Liam was born.

Liam grew up on a surfboard in Australia. Now he takes to the slopes on a snowboard too!

AUSSIE WONDER

Liam Hemsworth was born in Melbourne, Australia, where his mother, Leonie, was an English teacher and his father, Craig, was a social services counselor. When Liam was 13, the family moved to Phillip Island, off the coast of Australia. Phillip Island is pretty small, with fewer than 10,000 year-round residents, but—fortunately for Liam—it's also an excellent surfing spot. Liam spent a lot of time surfing with his brothers when he was growing up. He still tries to catch the waves whenever he can.

Liam *says:*

"The beaches of L.A. are more crowded than where I grew up on Phillip Island, but I think it's helped me to adjust to life in America—getting into the water as much as possible."

(*Interview* magazine)

Liam with his mother, Leonie, and brother Luke.

Liam and Chris in Hollywood.

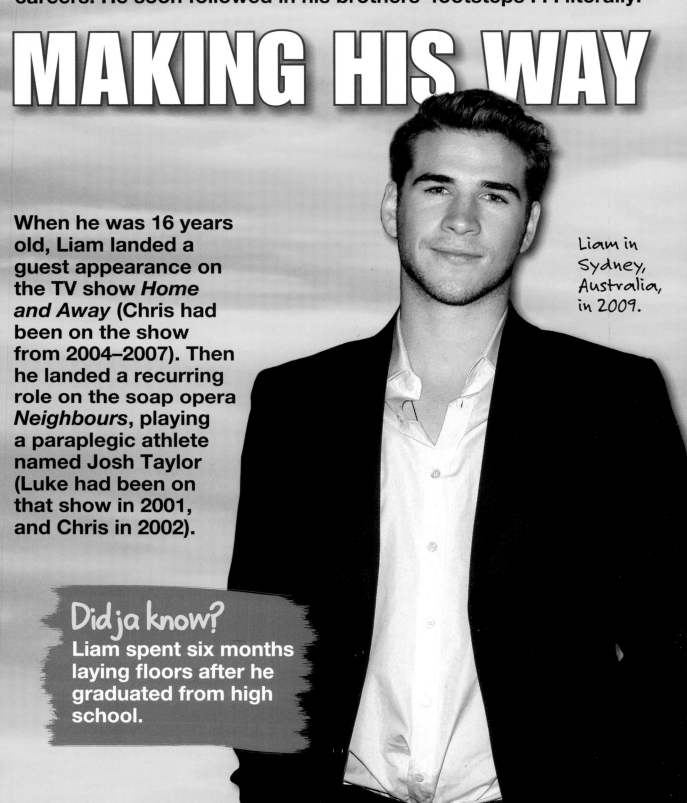

Liam first started acting in high school plays while his older brothers Luke and Chris were already pursuing their acting careers. He soon followed in his brothers' footsteps . . . literally.

MAKING HIS WAY

When he was 16 years old, Liam landed a guest appearance on the TV show *Home and Away* (Chris had been on the show from 2004–2007). Then he landed a recurring role on the soap opera *Neighbours*, playing a paraplegic athlete named Josh Taylor (Luke had been on that show in 2001, and Chris in 2002).

Liam in Sydney, Australia, in 2009.

Didja know?
Liam spent six months laying floors after he graduated from high school.

Guy Pearce (Iron Man 3), Simon Baker (The Mentalist), and Isla Fisher (The Great Gatsby) also appeared on the Aussie TV show Home and Away early in their careers.

Spice Girl Emma Bunton appeared in Neighbours too.

MODEL BEHAVIOR

Jen has been in front of the camera even longer than she's been acting on screen. A photographer in her hometown of Louisville, Kentucky, named Chris Kaufman shot some of her earliest professional photographs. Hats off to Jen—she was a natural talent at age 14.

Not all of Jen's modelling gigs went so well. She told talk show host Conan O'Brien about one of her biggest opportunities. "I did stuff for Abercrombie & Fitch, but you'd never know because none of my pictures ever got released," Jen revealed. Why not? While the other models at the shoot were pretending to catch the football in cute poses, Jen was actually trying to play football, tackling the other models. Unfortunately, this didn't make for great photos, though it does make for a great story.

Jen at 14.

Did ja know?

Jennifer Lawrence isn't the only *Hunger Games* actor who modelled for Abercrombie & Fitch. Alexander Ludwig (Cato) and Alan Ritchson (Gloss) did too.

Leven Rambin modelled for the "Sweet Valley High" book covers—as both twins, Jessica and Elizabeth. She also played look-alike half sisters on the soap opera *All My Children*.

PICTURE PERFECT!

Amandla Stenberg got her start in front of the camera as a catalog model for Disney when she was just four years old. No wonder she looks so comfortable in front of a camera!

TEEN TRIUMPHS

Outer space? Check. Inner Earth? Check. Dystopian future, flying fairy, troubled teen? Check, check, check. Josh has soared through the stars, met imaginary creatures, and acted alongside some of the hottest actors in Hollywood. Before he turned 20, Josh had been in more than a dozen films and numerous TV shows. Here are some faves.

Josh says:

"I love doing roles and movies that are different from each other. That's kind of why I like to be an actor, because I get to play different characters and pretend I'm different people going through different situations."

(Movieweb.com)

Goal! Josh scored a role as a young soccer player aside funnyman Will Ferrell in *Kicking and Screaming* (2005). Josh loves playing soccer in real life too!

In Zathura, Josh co-stars with Jonah Bobo and Twilight's Kristen Stewart as siblings caught up in a board game that leads them to a science-fiction space adventure.

Star power! In 2006, Josh teamed up with Robin Williams in the funny and touching family movie RV.

MAKING AN IMPACT

In 2007, Josh starred alongside AnnaSophia Robb in *Bridge to Terabithia*. The movie is based on the timeless children's book by Katherine Paterson—it won the Newbery Medal for Best Children's Book in 1978.

Filming this story about two lonely children who create a magical kingdom as an escape was an emotional experience for Josh. "The emotional scenes can be a challenge. There was some sadness but you use your emotions and what helped me was asking myself how I would really feel and act as if I were this character," Josh told Dove.org. Bridge to Terabithia won numerous awards, and Josh received a Young Artist Award for his work on the film.

There were fun times on set too— especially when they got to do some stuntwork while filming the battle scene with all the creatures of Terabithia. "You have to pretend you're swinging this stick at an amazing, crazy, creature thing that's attacking you and you have to be afraid of it when there's nothing there at all. It takes some imagining but we pulled it off, I think," Josh told Movieweb.com.

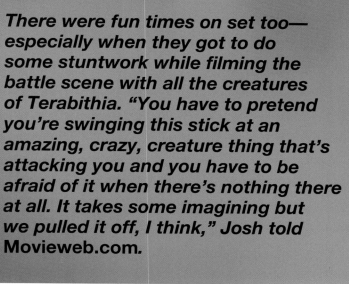

"I love doing independent films. I love being in the freezing cold with the rest of the crew, and the only thing that's keeping you there and motivating you is . . . not money . . . it's just the belief in a story that you love enough to do anything f And passion—that's why I do what I do."

That's what Jen said when she received the Independent S Award for Best Actress for her role as Tiffany, a recently wido young woman with an unpredictable personality, in *Silver Linir Playbook*. She wowed the world with her performance opposit Bradley Cooper. *Entertainment Weekly* called her performanc 'fabulous" and "incandescent"!

JEN'S INDEPENDENT SPIRIT

Bradley Cooper (Pat
Jacki Weaver (Delor
Chris Tucker (Danny
Jennifer Lawrence
(Tiffany), director
David O. Russell, Anu
Kher (Dr. Cliff Patel)

Awarding times: Jen won an Academy Award, Golden Globe Award, Screen Actors Guild Award, Satellite Award, MTV Movie Award, and People's Choice Award for her work in Silver Linings Playbook. She is the youngest person ever to be nominated for two Academy Awards for Best Actress, and the second-youngest Best Actress winner.

A sign of good things to come? Jen was on hand in the early morning hours on January 24, 2012, to help announce the Academy Award nominations. A year later, she'd hear her own name announced at the Oscars ceremony for Best Performance by an Actress in a Leading Role.

WINTER'S BONE

Jen really wanted the role of 17-year-old Ree Dolly in *Winter's Bone*, but when she first auditioned she was passed up because she was thought to be too pretty for the part. But that didn't stop Jen. She told *People* she showed up for another audition after taking the red-eye (an overnight flight). "Not brushing my hair or washing my face did the trick," she said.

In the movie Jen plays a teenage girl from a dirt-poor family who has a lot of responsibilities—looking after her younger sister, caring for her mentally ill mother, and hunting down her absent father in order to save her family home in the rural Ozark Mountains of the United States.

Actors Charlotte Jeane Lucas, Kevin Breznahan, Casey MacLaren, Tate Taylor, Jennifer Lawrence, Cody Brown, Lauren Sweetser, John Hawkes, Dale Dickey, and director Debra Granik pose for a portrait during the 2010 Sundance Film Festival.

The movie debuted at the Sundance Film Festival in 2010, and it won the Grand Jury Prize for Dramatic Film. It also received four Academy Award nominations: Best Picture, Best Adapted Screenplay, Best Actress (Go Jen!), and Best Supporting Actor. Jen was recognized for her work in the movie with the Academy Award nomination, as well as nominations for a Golden Globe Award, Satellite Award, Independent Spirit Award, and Screen Actors Guild Award for Best Actress.

Jen says:

"The only reason we were all out there in the freezing cold was because we loved the project. I love that feeling, that desperate, almost pathetic feeling of 'Are we actually going to be able to pull this off?'"

(*Vanity Fair*)

"Her performance is more than acting . . . Lawrence's eyes are a roadmap to what's tearing Ree apart."

(*Rolling Stone*)

LIAM ON THE RISE

When Liam moved to America in 2009 to pursue acting, it wasn't easy at first. He was cast in Sylvester Stallone's film *The Expendables*, but his character was ultimately written out of the script. Talk about expendable! But Liam later appeared in *The Expendables 2*, so things worked out after all.

    The Expendables 2 features Liam alongside action-movie royalty, including Sylvester Stallone, Jet Li, Chuck Norris, Bruce Willis, Jean-Claude Van Damme, and Arnold Schwarzenegger. That is one seriously star-studded cast!

Life-size Liam alongside his *The Expendables 2* co-stars.

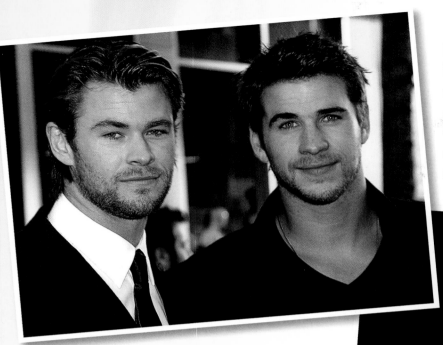

Liam auditioned for the lead in *Thor*, but the role went to his brother Chris. No hard feelings, as the brothers celebrated Chris's success at the movie's premiere.

Liam was recognized with a Breakthrough of the Year Award in 2010 by Young Hollywood Awards. He was thrilled —he said "thank you" seven times in his acceptance speech.

WE ♥ THE EXPENDABLES

Fans eagerly await the star-studded and hunky cast!

PERFECT HARMONY

Long walks on the beach, gorgeous sunsets, growing up, and falling in love . . . that could describe Liam's next movie, as well as the relationship that developed between Liam and his beautiful co-star, Miley Cyrus. *The Last Song*, a romantic coming-of-age story set on Tybee Island off the coast of Georgia, was Liam's break-out role. Filmed in the summer of 2009, *The Last Song* brought Liam and Miley together on screen . . . and off.

Liam says:

"From the first time we read, it was like I had known her before."

(*Teen Vogue*)

Liam and Miley's on-screen chemistry turned into an off-screen romance, and they made a gorgeous couple on the red carpet for *The Last Song* premiere.

Liam told *Collider.com*, "Volleyball was the hardest thing I've ever had to do. . . . I turned up for the first day of volleyball practice and I was honestly really scared to shoot the volleyball part because it takes a lot of skills to play that game and I didn't have them, at all."

In The Last Song, *Liam plays Will Blakelee, a volleyball player who volunteers at the local aquarium. Miley plays Ronnie Miller, a rebellious 17-year-old piano prodigy whose mother sends her to the small island community for the summer to reconnect with her father—they've been estranged since her parents got divorced a few years earlier. The characters first meet when Will runs into Ronnie—literally!—during a beach volleyball game, and they begin to grow close when they join forces to guard a sea turtle nest to protect the eggs from predators.*

FURRY FRIENDS
On Screen and Off

Josh and his *Firehouse Dog* co-star. Who's got the shaggier "do"?

Willow *says*:

"I have three dogs, a cat, and fish. I also used to have chickens, so you can see how much I love animals."

(*Twist*)

Josh adopted a pit bull puppy that had been dropped off at an animal shelter as a stray. He named the puppy Driver, after the movie *Drive*. "I always thought it was a good name for a dog," he told *Us Weekly*.

Didja know?

Is it possible that Jen's cat Cleo and Josh's dog Driver are on Twitter? Here's a recent exchange:
Driver Hutcherson: "Cleo! I've heard so much about you . . . hope I meet you one day."
Cleo Lawrence: "Hope to get to know you better, you seem to be one cool dog." Bet they have some help with the tweets!

Liam walks his dog Ziggy—although from the looks of things, Ziggy may be leading the way.

JENNIFER LAWRENCE IS KATNISS

Jen smiles thoughtfully on the set of The Hunger Games.

CASTING KATNISS:

Casting the role of Katniss in *The Hunger Games* was a job that would decide the fate of the movie series. Director Gary Ross needed someone whose maturity and screen presence would captivate an entire audience and make them believe that Katniss could really change the world. Who would fit the bill?

MOM KNOWS BEST

Jen told Fabulous *magazine that she took three days to decide whether or not she would take on the role of Katniss Everdeen, and every day she had a different answer. The project's intense fan base seemed intimidating. Then her mom set her straight. "Every time people ask you why you don't do studio movies, you always*

say that it's because you don't care about the size of the movie, you care about the story and the character…now you have a story and a character that you love, but you're not saying yes to it because of the size of it." The Hunger Games *is such a great story, and Katniss Everdeen is such an awesome character, Jen had to say yes!*

Gary Ross said casting Jennifer Lawrence was the easiest casting decision he ever made. Katniss "is a girl who needs to incite a revolution," Ross said, and Jennifer's audition was stunning.
(Entertainment Weekly)

JOSH HUTCHERSON IS PEETA

Josh with crew members on the set of *Catching Fire*.

Josh says:

"Peeta is all about staying true to yourself. He goes into the Games and does everything he can to maintain what he believes in and not become just another pawn."

(Parade)

CASTING PEETA

Josh auditioned for the role of Peeta, first meeting with director Gary Ross and *The Hunger Games* author Suzanne Collins. "Three lines into his audition and I knew he'd be fantastic," Suzanne Collins told *Entertainment Weekly*. Josh got called back to do a reading with Jennifer Lawrence to see how their characters would connect. And then Josh says he waited "a painful two weeks" to find out if he got the part. When he heard he was going to be Peeta, he was so happy he was speechless.

Didja know?

Alexander Ludwig also auditioned for the role of Peeta before being cast as Cato instead.

PEETA PERFECT

Josh related to Peeta's character and his fashion sense. In the scene where Peeta throws Katniss a loaf of bread, Josh got to wear a pair of work boots that he loved. "The boots and heavy material are kind of my style."

(People)

LIAM HEMSWORTH
IS GALE HAWTHORNE

Liam says:

"When I read the books, I always related to Gale." Perfect casting!

(*Sugarcape.com*)

Didja know?

Liam ran lines with his older brother and fellow actor Chris for his audition for *The Hunger Games*— Chris played the role of Katniss.

Playing Gale—a teenage hunter who lost his father in a mining accident, just like Katniss—brought Liam Hemsworth's acting style into the Hollywood limelight. Liam is quiet and powerful onscreen. He describes his acting style as "less is more."

"My biggest thing is just being present, and being able to react to what's happening. And working with Jennifer Lawrence . . . she's more present than anyone. It just becomes so real." (*Philstar.com*)

Liam really connected with the character he played. Gale "is extremely passionate about standing up for what he believes in, and that has always been a strong part of my life," Liam told *Vman.com*. He says filming the reaping scene was the toughest day on set, because it made him think about what it would feel like if *The Hunger Games* were real.

SAM CLAFLIN IS FINNICK ODAIR

CASTING CALL:

When Sam was first called in to read for the movie, he had no idea what part or film he was auditioning for. He was handed a script and saw the name Finnick Odair, but he hadn't read *The Hunger Games* books, so that didn't clue him in. Then he saw there was a character named Katniss. Got it!

Just like his *The Hunger Games: Catching Fire* co-star Donald Sutherland, Sam studied at the London Academy of Music and Dramatic Art. And guess what? He began his acting career in the television mini-series *Pillars of the Earth*, which also featured Donald Sutherland. In a subsequent film, Sam showed off his action-movie skills in *Pirates of the Caribbean: On Stranger Tides*, playing a character who risks his life to rescue the mermaid he has fallen in love with.

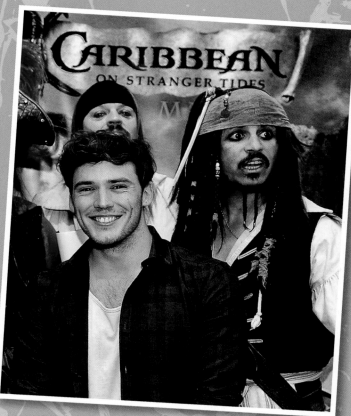

At a *Pirates of the Caribbean: On Stranger Tides* event.

Sam starred in *Snow White and the Huntsman* as the dark prince, and Liam Hemsworth's brother Chris was the huntsman.

WILLOW SHIELDS
IS PRIMROSE EVERDEEN

Willow Shields lights up the screen as Katniss's sister, Primrose Everdeen. She won praise for her acting abilities—and her ability to cry on demand helped her portray Prim's emotional journey. *The Hunger Games* director Gary Ross told *Entertainment Weekly*, "We're very lucky to have her."

Willow's older brother, River, and twin sister, Autumn, are also actors. She had a wonderful on-screen big sis too—Jennifer Lawrence was a mentor to her and to Amandla Stenberg (who plays Rue). Willow said, "The advice that she gave us is really incredible!" (*The Hot Hits*)

Full name: **Willow Shields**
Birth date: **June 1, 2000**
Zodiac sign: **Gemini**
Born in: **Albuquerque, New Mexico**

Didja know?

Willow has lots of interests. In addition to being a talented young actress, she spends her free time making art, and loves history and reading.

Full name: **Paula Malcomson**
Born in: **1970**
Born in: **Belfast, Northern Ireland, UK**
Moved to the United States: **1991**

Didja know?

Paula played Jen's mom before *The Hunger Games*. In 2007, the two starred as a mother-daughter team in an episode of the television series *Cold Case*.

PAULA MALCOMSON
IS MRS. EVERDEEN

Paula Malcomson chuckled with *E!* that to prepare for her role as Katniss and Prim's mom, she just lay in bed depressed for a month before heading to the set. But there was much more to it than that. Producer Nina Jacobson said the role needed an actress "who could transport herself, and audiences, to a place as tough as District 12." (*Entertainment Weekly*)

Paula has had a very busy career, with roles in many films and television series. One of her early roles was in the family film *Dunston Checks In*, which also starred an orangutan! She also acted in the hit television show *Lost*. When she's not acting, she loves to read, sleep, and cook.

ELIZABETH BANKS IS EFFIE TRINKET

Full name: Elizabeth Maresal Mitchell (Elizabeth Banks is her stage name.)
Birth date: February 10, 1974
Zodiac sign: Aquarius
Born in: Pittsfield, Massachusetts

Elizabeth Banks's sense of style and humor come across in all her movies. In *Seabiscuit* she plays Marcela Howard, a character she describes as really outspoken and very sassy. That could describe Effie, as well! Gary Ross directed *Seabiscuit*, so when Elizabeth heard that he was chosen as the director of *The Hunger Games*, she sent him an email suggesting that she would make a good Effie.

Didja know?

Elizabeth recorded herself trying out different accents for Effie and sent them to director Gary Ross in order to perfect Effie's prissy Capitol accent.

Like many of *The Hunger Games* actors, Donald Sutherland got an early start, working at a local radio station when he was 14 years old. He studied some acting in college, and took it up in earnest when he moved to London to attend the London Academy of Music and Dramatic Art. He brought the iconic role of Hawkeye Pierce to life in the 1970 movie *M*A*S*H*, and his many roles in films and on television have won him numerous awards and honors, including two Golden Globe Awards. He also garnered a Role Model Award in 2008 from the Young Hollywood Awards in Los Angeles.

As Merrick Jamison-Smythe in the popular movie *Buffy the Vampire Slayer*, Donald played alongside a teenage heroine who saved a town, and maybe the world: a little like Katniss!

Full name: Donald McNichol Sutherland
Birth date: July 17, 1935
Zodiac sign: Cancer
Born in: Saint John, New Brunswick, Canada

Didja know?

Donald Sutherland's son Keifer Sutherland plays action hero Jack Bauer in the TV series *24*. Powerful actors run in the family!

DONALD SUTHERLAND IS PRESIDENT CORIOLANUS SNOW

WES BENTLEY
IS SENECA CRANE

Full name: Wesley Cook Bentley
Birth date: September 4, 1978
Zodiac sign: Virgo
Born in: Jonesboro, Arkansas

Before tackling the character of Seneca Crane, the controlling gamemaker in the Arena, Juilliard-trained Wes was known for his breakout role as Ricky Fitts in the Oscar winning film *American Beauty*. How did Wes approach his *Hunger Games* character? "He's only evil in that he's ignorant . . . I don't think he knows the full consequences of what he's doing." (*Access Hollywood*)

Didja know?

Seneca Crane's beard was Wes's own—it took about two hours each day he was filming to get the beard trimmed and shaped.

STANLEY TUCCI IS CAESAR FLICKERMAN

This award-winning actor brings dramatic flair to the role of Caesar Flickerman. "I liked the story a lot. I liked what it has to say for socio-political reasons. I like the fact that the lead character is this incredible, strong young woman." (*WSJ Speakeasy*) Other recent movies include *Percy Jackson: Sea of Monsters* and *Captain America: The First Avenger*.

Full name: Stanley Tucci
Birth date: November 11, 1960
Zodiac sign: Scorpio
Born in: Peekskill, New York

PHILIP SEYMOUR HOFFMAN IS PLUTARCH HEAVENSBEE

Full name: Philip Seymour Hoffman
Birth date: July 23, 1967
Zodiac sign: Leo
Born in: Fairport, New York

A critically acclaimed stage and screen actor, Philip won an Oscar for his starring role in *Capote*. "Actors are responsible to the people we play. I don't label or judge. I just play them as honestly and expressively and creatively as I can," he told *Time*. This bodes well for his performance as the head gamekeeper in *Catching Fire*.

LENNY KRAVITZ
IS CINNA

Full name: Leonard Albert Kravitz
Birth date: May 26, 1964
Zodiac sign: Gemini
Born in: New York, New York

Didja know?

Jen and Lenny's daughter, Zoe, were in *X-Men: First Class* together.

Singer and songwriter Lenny Kravitz came to director Gary Ross's attention for the caring character he played in the movie *Precious*. And his approach to Cinna, the stylist for the District 12 team who did his best for Katniss, was understated and classic. What was *The Hunger Games* experience like for Lenny? "What I came away with is that it's just so satisfying to do a great project with great people. Every day was fun." (*Collider.com*)

Woody Harrelson has had an impressive acting career, from his iconic role as Woody Boyd on the long-running television series *Cheers*, for which he won an Emmy Award, to the 2013 film *Now You See Me*, which also stars Mark Ruffalo (who co-starred with Josh Hutcherson in *The Kids Are All Right*). Of his experience playing Katniss and Peeta's mentor Haymitch, Woody told *Moviefone.com*, "I was really happy to do it because what a great experience it was to be hanging out with this cool group of people. . . . Just the level of talent from every department, outstanding."

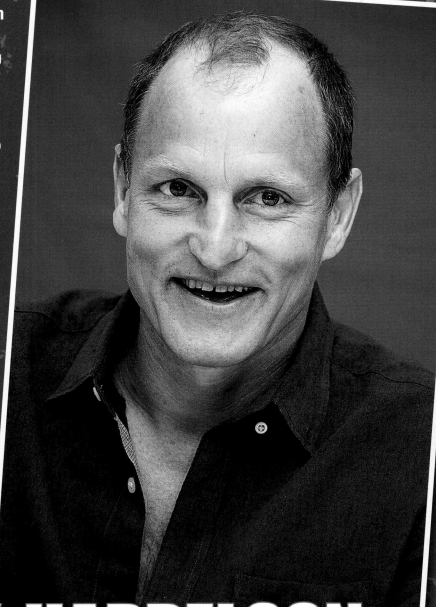

WOODY HARRELSON
IS HAYMITCH ABERNATHY

Full name: **Woodrow Tracy Harrelson**
Birth date: **July 23, 1961**
Zodiac sign: **Leo**
Born in: **Midland, Texas**

AMANDLA STENBERG
IS RUE

Full name: Amandla Stenberg
Birth date: October 23, 1998
Zodiac sign: Libra
Born in: Los Angeles, California

Didja know?

Amandla is a Zulu word that means "power."

Amandla says:

"Rue's very musical and she's very quick and she's very sweet. And I think I have some of those qualities. I'm very musical—I play violin, drums, and guitar and I like to sing so I think I relate to Rue in that way."

(Twist)

Amandla loves to read, so this bookstore fan event was perfect for her!

LEVEN RAMBIN IS GLIMMER

Full name: Leven Rambin
Birth date: May 17, 1990
Zodiac sign: Taurus
Born in: Houston, Texas

Leven says:

The Hunger Games is "not just any movie, it's my favorite book being a movie, and a huge one at that. I'm excited to be a part of something so much bigger than myself."

(Interview)

JACK QUAID IS MARVEL

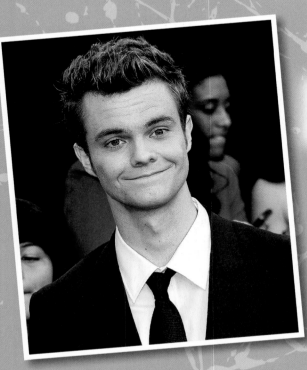

Full name: Jack Henry Quaid
Birth date: April 24, 1992
Zodiac sign: Taurus
Born in: Los Angeles, California
Showbiz start: Jack was born into the biz—his parents are Hollywood legends Dennis Quaid and Meg Ryan—but playing Marvel in *The Hunger Games* is his first movie role. "I've been on sets all my life," he told *Us Weekly*, "but this is the first time I wasn't . . . [on] the sidelines."

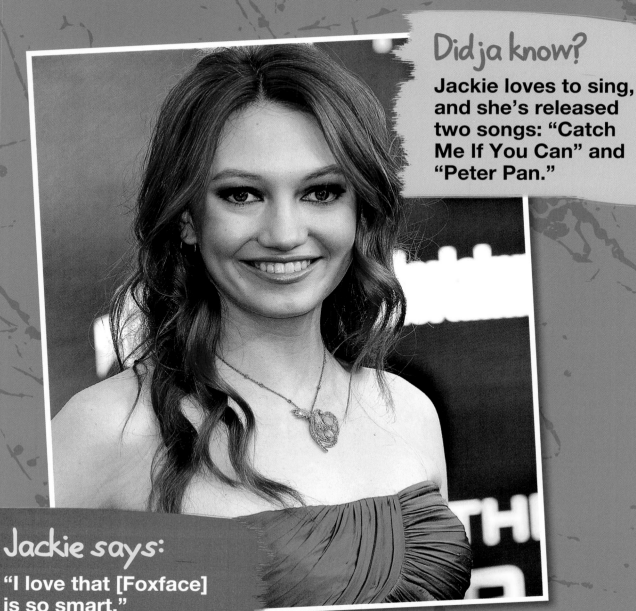

Did ja know?

Jackie loves to sing, and she's released two songs: "Catch Me If You Can" and "Peter Pan."

Jackie says:

"I love that [Foxface] is so smart."

(Seventeen.com)

JACQUELINE EMERSON
IS FOXFACE

Full name: Jacqueline Bonnell Marteau Emerson
Goes by: Jackie
Birth date: August 21, 1994
Zodiac sign: Leo
Born in: Washington, DC

DAYO OKENIYI
IS THRESH

Full name: Oladayo. A. Okeniyi
Birth date: June 14, 1988
Zodiac sign: Gemini
Born in: Jos, Nigeria, Africa

Dayo says:

"Without Thresh, there is no second movie. Katniss would have died if Thresh didn't save her, so I think that was my favorite scene."

(Seventeen.com)

ISABELLE FUHRMAN IS CLOVE

Full name: **Isabelle Fuhrman**
Birth date: **February 25, 1997**
Zodiac sign: **Pisces**
Born in: **Washington, DC**

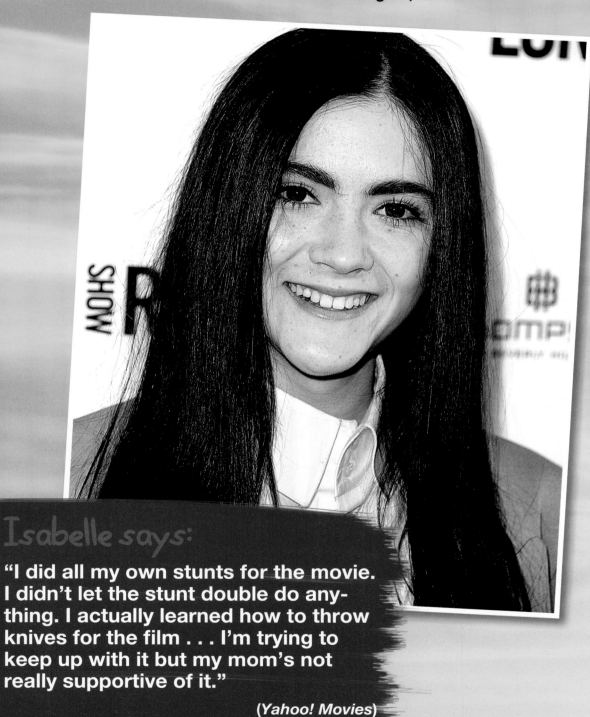

Isabelle says:

"I did all my own stunts for the movie. I didn't let the stunt double do anything. I actually learned how to throw knives for the film . . . I'm trying to keep up with it but my mom's not really supportive of it."

(Yahoo! Movies)

Zxander says:

"I'm always playing the nice guy, and it's fun playing the bad guy once in a while. I got to really experiment with a side of me that I've never seen before and definitely the audience hasn't seen before."

(Bullettmedia.com)

ALEXANDER LUDWIG
IS CATO

Full name: Alexander Ludwig
Goes by: Zxander
Birth date: May 7, 1992
Zodiac sign: Taurus
Born in: Vancouver, British Columbia, Canada

FAN-DEMONIUM

Long before *The Hunger Games* movie came out, people everywhere fell in love with the story and devoted fans wanted to be the first to see Katniss, Peeta, and Gale brought to life on the big screen. Movie premieres are usually exclusive celebrity events, but the producers wanted to include the fans, too, and they came up with an amazing plan. Four hundred lucky fans won tickets to the premiere and exclusive privileges to camp out while they waited for the movie to open in a special area near the Nokia Theater in Los Angeles, where the premiere would be taking place. The fan camp, called "The Hob" after the District 12 marketplace in the story, was decorated with homemade signs and banners and had a party atmosphere. The odds were in their favor as these lucky fans attended the premiere and an amazing afterparty in a big tent decorated like the Capitol. A dream come true!

That's one lucky fan posing for a photo with Josh!

Fans give Josh and Jen the District 12 salute.

Ecstatic fans lean over the barricade to get Jen's picture and autograph.

Wes flashes a winning smile while signing autographs.

The Hunger Games was an international sensation, and the stars of the movie met their fans at premieres around the world. Wherever they went, the actors discovered that everyone had at least one thing in common: they love *The Hunger Games* movie and stars!

GOING GLOBAL

A fan snaps a pic with Zxander in Toronto, Canada.

Fans dressed as Capitol characters smile big on their way to the opening night of the film in New York City.

Jen autographs for a fan in Madrid, Spain, where they call their favorite film *Los Juegos del Hambre*.

British fans go crazy at the London premiere!

COMIC-CON 2013

Founded by fans of comics, movies, and science fiction, Comic-Con has grown into a huge event held every summer in San Diego, California. This convention brings celebrities and creators of cool content together with their fans for a weekend of fun panels, advance launches for new movies and video games, and tons of cool costumes.

Some of the cast, including new members Jeffrey Wright and Jena Malone, together for a group photo.

It's no surprise that the stars of the eagerly awaited The Hunger Games: Catching Fire *made a big splash at the Comic-Con 2013. Fans got a sneak peek at the new movie trailer, heard the stars speak onstage, collected autographs, and snapped photos with their favorites.*

A lucky fan dressed as Katniss got to ask the panel a question. What would you ask Jen, Josh, and Liam?

Red Carpet
GOLD

When Jennifer Lawrence rocketed to superstardom, she felt just like her character, Katniss. "Katniss was a girl who's all of a sudden being introduced to fame. I know what that feels like," she told *Entertainment Weekly*.

Jen dazzles on the red carpet at the world premiere of The Hunger Games *in Los Angeles.*

GLAM JEWELS

No sign of jet lag as Jen gives English fans a thrill at the London movie premiere.

FIERCE SHOES

Red Carpet
HUNKS . . .

Life in the Hollywood fast lane means lots of events, and often a different outfit for each one. Stars have help, of course—stylists who do everything from helping their clients figure out a style that suits them, to making them look awesome at a major event, and even picking out everyday clothing like jeans and T-shirts. But the best red carpet style reflects the actor's own fashion sense and savvy, for a look that is perfect . . . and perfectly theirs.

Josh loves his casual jeans, flannels, and boots, but when it's time to hit the red carpet he's ready to rock it in style. "I love getting dressed up doing the whole premiere look," Josh told the Los Angeles Times. Of course he has stylists who help him get red carpet–ready, but he makes the final decisions. "Everything I wear is very much what I want to wear, it's not just a matter of someone handing you clothes and saying: 'Here, play dress up.'"

Sam Claflin looking picture-perfect at the premiere of Snow White and the Huntsman.

Sam says:

"I'm just not that into fashion." You could have fooled us!

(Hungertv.com)

Liam's look for The Hunger Games: Catching Fire Cannes Party—très beau!

HOTTIES....

Lenny's passion for fashion is reflected in the cool clothes that his character, Cinna, wears. Impressed by the costume designer, Lenny said that in Catching Fire, "I felt like I was wearing my own things."

(Hitfix.com)

Wes Bentley sports a textured, dapper look at The Hunger Games premiere. No elaborate Seneca facial hair here!

Alan Ritchson (left) and Dayo Okeniyi (right) show their personal style when they hit the red carpet.

...AND GORGEOUS GALS!

Elizabeth Banks pulls off a stunning strapless gown at the 2013 Vanity Fair Oscar Party.

Willow and Amandla show off their fashion savvy at The Hunger Games premiere.

Isabelle Fuhrman

Jena was nominated for a Screen Actors Guild Award when she was only 12 years old—the first of many nominations and wins. No wonder she looks so comfortable on the red carpet!

Leven was totally into fashion as a teen, and she loved going to fashion shows. She told *Seventeen* she was "a downtown glamorous girl" at 17—looks like she still is!

ACTING CLASS

Many actors say they always knew they wanted to be on stage, and school is a great place to get started. These yearbook photos show how some of your favorites from *The Hunger Games* got their start.

Julianne Moore, who is slated to play District 13 rebellion leader President Alma Coin in *The Hunger Games: Mockingjay*, got her start in a high school play.

Elizabeth Banks showed her theatrical side early. Doesn't this costume remind you of a certain Capitol fashionista she would go on to play?

Lenny Kravitz already looked like a rock star during his time in the music program at Beverly Hills High School.

It looks like Wes Bentley enjoyed mugging for the camera from an early age, though this playful boy is a far cry from serious gamemaker Seneca Crane.

SHAPING UP

How do you get into shape to be strong enough to fight in the arena, but stay lean enough to look like hunger is your biggest concern? The actors in *The Hunger Games* had to work hard to slim down and muscle up for the movie.

Jen talked to MTV about her training routine, which included rock climbing, tree climbing, running, and vaulting. She trained in archery with Olympic archer Khatuna Lorig.

Liam had to lose weight and slim down his big muscles to look like a deprived District 12 resident. He trained with an ex–Navy SEAL Logan Hood, and his workout included flipping tires and hitting a body bag with a baseball bat. He got extra motivation from his brother Chris, who sent him a text message suggesting that he needed to slim down: "It's called The Hunger Games, *not* The Eating Games!" *(Men's Health)*

Josh had to look lean, but he also needed to bulk up to have the upper body strength his character required—Peeta lifted flour bags at his family's bakery at the beginning of the story. To achieve this look, Josh put in five one-hour workouts a week and added 15 pounds to his frame. Josh's trainer, Bobby Strom, told Men's Fitness, "Josh puts in 100 percent in his career, and 100 percent at the gym, too."

Alexander Ludwig, who plays career tribute Cato, had to bulk up too, adding 30-plus pounds of muscle to his frame for the role. Zxander told Entertainment Weekly that the whole cast worked out together between filming, flipping tires, climbing ropes, and having races. They all built camaraderie and muscle at the same time!

Liam spent a lot of time surfing with his brothers Chris and Luke when he was growing up. And he surfed competitively for five years, from the age of 13. He even had a class about surfing at school! How important was surfing to young Liam? "I did it every day, in the morning and after school," Liam told *Men's Health* magazine. He still tries to catch the waves whenever he can.

WONDERS DOWN UNDER

Liam, his brothers Chris and Luke, and their father Craig still take surfing trips together, and were photgraphed catching the waves in Costa Rica early in 2013. Cowabunga, dudes!

SCORE!

Josh has loved playing sports since he was a little kid, when he began playing soccer in his Kentucky hometown.

Josh keeps up with his mad soccer skills between scenes on movie sets and in his spare time. He and *Catching Fire* co-star Sam Claflin played during filming breaks, and Josh has played soccer across the globe, kicking with pals in Atlanta's Piedmont Park, with a rookie team in Italy, and in a BritWeek celebrity game in Canada.

Josh says:

"I'm more star-struck by athletes than actors."

(Now)

Josh is into other sports too! Here he is catching air time against the pros in the NBA All-Star Celebrity Game in 2013.

Josh shares a moment with his brother, Connor, at a game between the Miami Marlins and his beloved Cincinnati Reds. Josh got to throw out the first pitch. Wow!

CO-STAR CHEMISTRY

Sometimes the on-screen chemistry that lights up a movie screen leads to an off-screen friendship. And sometimes it ignites a romantic spark. Maybe it's the emotional storyline of a movie, the intense hours together on a movie set far away from home, or simply fate that conspires to bring two actors together in real life.

Raven (aka Mystique) and Hank McCoy (aka Beast) in a scene from X-Men: First Class.

Jen got to know her X-Men: First Class co-star Nicholas Hoult on the set of the movie in 2010. They began dating, but in January 2013, the couple split. They've been spotted together since— and they appeared at Comic-Con 2013 to promote their upcoming film X-Men: Days of Future Past, coming in 2014. Just friends . . . or something more?

Liam's on-screen relationship with Miley Cyrus in The Last Song led to off-screen romance. When they got engaged in 2012, Miley tweeted, "I'm so happy to be engaged and look forward to a life of happiness with @LiamHemsworth!!! I feel like all my dreams are coming true. Life is beautiful." (BBC.co.uk) Like many relationships, they've had their ups and downs. Is their on-again, off-again relationship on . . . or off? Only the two of them know for sure.

Jen and Nicholas having fun in Monte Carlo, Monaco, in 2012.

ROMANTIC TIMES

What's Josh looking for in a in a romantic partner? He told *Seventeen* magazine, "I like girls I can have deep conversations with. The meaning of life and existence—you can go on forever about that stuff." He found what he was looking for in his *Journey 2: The Mysterious Island* co-star, Vanessa Hudgens. They tried to keep mum about their relationship, which worked until an interviewer on the Australian television show *Today* asked them about it—after they'd broken up. Awkward! Josh's new leading lady is his on-screen romantic interest in *Paradise Lost*, Claudia Traisac. Such a gorgeous couple!

Josh and Vanessa on the red carpet at the Journey 2: The Mysterious Island premiere.

Josh met GF Claudia Traisac when they were filming Paradise Lost in 2013.

Romance in bloom at the Snow White and the Hunstman world premiere in London.

Sam Claflin is married to Laura Haddock. They met at an audition, and Sam says he knew right away that she was the one for him. After the audition, he called his agent and said, "'Mate, I am in love.' He's like, 'How did the audition go, mate?' I was like, 'No, no, you don't understand. I have just met the woman I want to marry.'" (*Cover Media/Viva Press*) Sounds like love at first sight!

JSL On S.N.L

Jen can play serious characters with award-winning sensitivity and grit, and she can also bring down the house with her sense of humor. When she hosted *Saturday Night Live*, Jen got to show off her funny bone in a show filled with hilarious skits.

In the promo for her appearance on S.N.L., Jen brought a bow and arrow, Katniss-style!

Jen rocked a punk attitude in the *Girlfriends Talk Show* skit.

Can you recognize Jen in her dog chef costume?
She's the one in the middle with the red bow and the blonde whiskers!

KIDDING AROUND

The stars of *The Hunger Games* have taken on the Hollywood tradition of on-set pranks. And everyone seems to be involved.

Woody says:

Jen is the funniest woman he knows. "I'm in a perpetual state of laughter with her, which is a pretty good way to be on set." (*USA Today*)

During a break in filming The Hunger Games, *Jen* dared Josh to catch a leech. Of course he accepted the dare—but the slimy, squirmy critter got stuck to his hand. Ew!

Leven got caught up in the action too. She told *Seventeen* about hiding the furniture in fellow actors' trailers.

Just like Rue, Amandla shouldn't be underestimated! She made her mark with prank phone calls to Zxander and some of the other cast members. That is, when she wasn't snagging and hiding other cast members' clothes. Quite the prankster!

AWARDING TIMES

The star-studded cast of *The Hunger Games* has won many awards for their work. At the 2013 Golden Globe Awards ceremony, Jen received the award for "Best Performance by an Actress in a Motion Picture—Musical or Comedy" for her role as recently widowed, unpredictable Tiffany Maxwell in *Silver Linings Playbook*.

Stanley Tucci has nabbed two *Golden Globes*, for his performances in Conspiracy *and* Winchell. *So has cast mate Donald Sutherland, for* Path to War *and* Citizen X.

Woody Harrelson received a Golden Globe Award for his role in The Messenger. He was nominated for his performance in the 2012 TV movie Game Change— Woody's co-star in that movie, Julianne Moore, won for her role as vice presidential candidate Sarah Palin. Look for Julianne in the upcoming Mockingjay.

WINNING WAYS

Jen won an Oscar for her role in Silver Linings Playbook; she was also nominated for an Oscar for her performance in Winter's Bone. She nabbed an Empire Award, an Independent Spirit Award, four MTV Movie Awards, a Kids' Choice Award, three People's Choice Awards, a Screen Actors Guild Award, and three Teen Choice Awards. Sounds like a lot, but we have a feeling Jen is just beginning!

YOUNG HOLLYWOOD AWARD

Elizabeth Banks won the Young Hollywood Award for Exciting New Face the same year she starred in Seabiscuit—and she was nominated for a Screen Actors Guild Award that year too. She's taken home two Emmys for her work on 30 Rock, and an MTV Movie Awards trophy for Best On-Screen Transformation for her metamorphosis into Effie Trinket. Fantastic!

MTV MOVIE AWARDS

Josh and Zxander look pretty friendly for two guys who just won MTV Movie Awards for Best Fight! Josh's shelf also includes several Young Artist Awards and Teen Choice Awards, including a Choice: Liplock Award for his on-screen kiss with Jen. Sweet!

TEEN CHOICE AWARDS

Zxander, Amandla, and Willow accepted a Nickelodeon Kids' Choice Award blimp on behalf of the whole team for Favorite Movie. Jen was also nominated for Favorite Actress and Favorite Female Butt Kicker!

KIDS' CHOICE AWARDS

The fans have spoken—Josh took home a surfboard in 2012 for Choice Movie Actor: Sci-Fi/Fantasy. The Hunger Games won for Choice Movie: Sci-Fi/Fantasy.

GOOD DEEDS

Many of the actors support many different charities and get involved in many different ways. Here are just a few—such inspiration!

Josh is one of the founders of Straight But Not Narrow, and was honored with a GLAAD Vanguard Award. GLAAD president Herndon Graddick said, "Josh's commitment to achieving equality for every American is a message he carries in his work both on screen and off." Josh's castmate Sam Claflin also participates in Straight But Not Narrow.

The Josh Hutcherson Celebrity Basketball Game raises awareness—and money!—for his charity, Straight But Not Narrow.

Jen and Willow support DoSomething.org, a national organization dedicated to getting young people involved in causes they believe in.

Amandla is a supporter of the Martin Luther King, Jr. Memorial Foundation. She gave a speech in front of thousands of people at the dedication of the Martin Luther King, Jr. Memorial in Washington, DC, when she was just 12 years old.

Amandla with Cicely Tyson at the dedication ceremony for the Martin Luther King, Jr. Memorial.

PARTY TIME!

What is the cast of *The Hunger Games* up to when they're not filming? It looks as though they have been having a lot of fun.

Amandla Stenberg acted fierce at this fang-tastic Camp Ronald McDonald for Good Times Halloween Carnival.

Stanley blew out the candles on a huge cake at the premiere of *Winchell* in 1998. If he wished for acting success, then wishes do come true!

Liam celebrated his 21st birthday with a birthday cake and a few friends.

Elizabeth had a sparkle-filled birthday party in Las Vegas.

BODACIOUS BEACH BODS!

Wherever there's a beach, you may find one of your favorite *Hunger Games* stars hanging ten—or just hanging out.

Josh goes paddleboarding in Hawaii.

Jen goes all-in while surfing in Hawaii.

Alexander Ludwig was too hot to handle at the Victoria's Secret PINK Ultimate Spring Break Dance Party in Miami.

WHAT'S NEXT?

What are the stars of *The Hunger Games* up to when they're not shooting a *Hunger Games* movie? Shooting other movies, of course!

Did ja know?

Jacqueline Emerson has something other than movies on the mind; she's going to attend Stanford University. What a brainiac!

Soon after The Hunger Games *movie was released, Leven Rambin and Stanley Tucci began filming 2013's* Percy Jackson: Sea of Monsters.

Elizabeth Banks is joining Will Ferrell, Morgan Freeman, Channing Tatum, and others in giving voice to the characters in the animated feature The Lego Movie, slated for release in 2014.

Sam Claflin is starring as the main love interest in the upcoming romantic comedy Love, Rosie alongside Lily Collins.

Willow Shields will star in 2014's adventure-fantasy movie called The Wonder, about a group of classmates who follow a rainbow and find themselves magically in China—and in danger!

Amandla Stenberg is the voice of Savannah in the animated movie Rio 2, due out in March 2014. Co-stars include Anne Hathaway and Jesse Eisenberg.

CATCHING FIRE

What was it like to shoot scenes from *Catching Fire* in Hawaii? Warm weather, tropical breezes, beautiful beaches . . . sounds amazing! There were also long days of shooting, and many hours spent in the water. The movie trailer gives a glimpse of the tropical arena where the tributes are launched into the 75th Hunger Games in *Catching Fire*. Spectacular!

The cast and crew during *Catching Fire* filming.

Lionsgate threw an elaborate Capitol-style party for *Catching Fire* at the Cannes Film Festival in France (May 2013). That sure is some big hair—Effie Trinket would be proud!

ALL-STAR UPDATE

Want more Jen, Josh, and Liam? Fear not—Hollywood is keeping these red-hot stars busy with exciting roles.

In Serena, *a film set during the Great Depression, Jen reunites on screen with her* Silver Linings Playbook *co-star Bradley Cooper.*

Jen returns as Mystique in the X-Men *sequel,* Days of Future Past, *with co-stars Hugh Jackman as Wolverine and Jen's ex Nicholas Hoult as Beast. (2014)*

Josh will reprise his role of Sean Anderson opposite Dwayne "The Rock" Johnson in the third film in the "Journey to the Center of the Earth" *franchise*, From the Earth to the Moon. *(2014)*

Liam has been busy *since* The Hunger Games, *starring in* Empire State, Love and Honor, *and* Paranoia.

SNAP SHOTS

History mystery! Jena Malone sports modern shades with her full Victorian dress on the set of independent period film *Angelica*.

Liam looks cool in the Australian heat on a visit home with Miley Cyrus.

Isabelle looks psyched to be in the front row at designer Christian Siriano's show during New York Fashion Week.

Zxander sneaks in a little shopping before his guest appearance on *Extra*.

Elizabeth Banks keeps it casually fashionable while shopping at a farmer's market in Los Angeles.

Josh dances his heart out with Vanessa Hudgens and Ashley Tisdale at the Elton John AIDS Foundation Academy Awards Viewing Party.

PHOTO CREDITS